Christine McFadden

pasta

simple and delicious easy-to-make recipes

This is a Parragon Book
This edition published in 2005

Parragon
Queen Street House
4 Queen Street
Bath BA1 1HE, UK

Copyright © Parragon 2001

ISBN: 1-40546-230-2

Printed in China

Produced by
THE BRIDGEWATER BOOK COMPANY LTD

Photographer Simon Punter
Home Economist Ricky Turner

Cover Photography Calvey Taylor-Haw
Home Economist Ruth Pollock

NOTES FOR THE READER

- This book uses both metric and imperial measurements. Follow the same units of measurement throughout; do not mix metric and imperial.

- All spoon measurements are level: teaspoons are assumed to be 5 ml, and tablespoons are assumed to be 15 ml.

- Unless otherwise stated, milk is assumed to be full fat, eggs and individual vegetables such as potatoes are medium, and pepper is freshly ground black pepper.

- Recipes using raw or very lightly cooked eggs should be avoided by infants, the elderly, pregnant women, convalescents, and anyone suffering from an illness.

- Optional ingredients, variations or serving suggestions have not been included in the calculations.

- The times given are an approximate guide only. Preparation times differ according to the techniques used by different people and the cooking times vary as a result of the type of oven used.

contents

introduction

Cooked in minutes and easy on the purse, pasta is one of the most versatile of foods, combining happily with a wide variety of sauces. Although meat-based sauces are among the best known, vegetables provide inspiration for many delicious sauces, as do fish and seafood.

Pasta comes in a large number of shapes: flat and round ribbons, tubes, quills and corkscrews, to name but a few. Each shape lends itself to a particular sauce style. For example, long, thin pasta, such as spaghetti, is best for tomato or oil-based sauces, which coat the surface and cling to it. Wide, flat ribbons, such as fettucine, go well with cream sauces. Shapes or short, hollow tubes are perfect for chunkier sauces because they trap tasty morsels in their crevices.

To cook perfect pasta, use a large pan so the pasta has enough room to move around freely. Allow 1 litre/1¾ pints of water for every 115 g/4 oz of pasta.

meat sauce with mushrooms & tomatoes
page 12

asparagus & gorgonzola sauce with cream
page 58

Bring the water to a fast boil, then add the salt and pasta together, stirring once. Cooking time depends on the type of pasta. It is ready when al dente – tender, but still firm to the bite and slightly chewy. Be careful not to overcook. It is generally better to cook the sauce before the pasta; sauces can be kept waiting, but pasta cannot – it becomes sticky!

easy

Recipes are graded as follows:
1 spoon = easy;
2 spoons = very easy;
3 spoons = extremely easy.

serves 4

Recipes generally serve four people. Simply halve the ingredients to serve two, taking care not to mix metric and imperial measurements.

15 minutes

Preparation time. Where marinating or soaking are involved, these times have been added on separately: eg, 15 minutes + 30 minutes to marinate.

40 minutes

Cooking time. Cooking times do not include the cooking of side dishes or accompaniments served with the main dishes.

prawn & garlic sauce with cream
page 78

tuna with garlic, lemon, capers & olives
page 86

Rich, hearty, meat-based sauces include the universally popular Bolognese, which needs no introduction. There are also irresistible sauces made with coarse-cut sausages or bacon and enriched with tomatoes, mushrooms or peppers. Less well-known are more delicate sauces made with chicken. These often include generous amounts of cream and freshly grated cheese for richness and flavour. All the sauces are simple to prepare and are equally suitable for relaxed entertaining or family suppers.

meat & poultry
sauces

classic bolognese meat sauce

very easy   serves 4

15 minutes   1 hour
             15 minutes

ingredients

2 tbsp olive oil

1 tbsp butter

1 small onion, chopped finely

1 carrot, chopped finely

1 celery stick, chopped finely

50 g/1¾ oz mushrooms, diced

225 g/8 oz minced beef

75 g/2¾ oz unsmoked bacon or ham, diced

2 chicken livers, chopped

2 tbsp tomato purée

125 ml/4 fl oz dry white wine

salt and pepper

½ tsp freshly grated nutmeg

300 ml/10 fl oz chicken stock

125 ml/4 fl oz double cream

450 g/1 lb dried spaghetti

2 tbsp chopped fresh parsley, to garnish

freshly grated Parmesan cheese, to serve

Heat the oil and butter in a large saucepan over a medium heat. Add the onion, carrot, celery and mushrooms to the pan, then fry until soft. Add the beef and bacon to the pan and fry until the beef is evenly browned.

Stir in the chicken livers and tomato purée and cook for 2–3 minutes. Pour in the wine and season with salt, pepper and the nutmeg. Add the stock. Bring to the boil, then cover and simmer gently over a low heat for 1 hour. Stir in the cream and simmer, uncovered, until reduced.

Cook the pasta in plenty of boiling salted water until al dente. Drain and transfer to a warm serving dish.

Pour half the sauce over the pasta. Toss well to mix. Spoon the remaining sauce over the top.

Garnish with the parsley and serve with Parmesan cheese.

macaroni with sausage, pepperoncini & olives

very easy   serves 4

10–15 minutes   15 minutes

ingredients

1 tbsp olive oil

1 large onion, chopped finely

2 garlic cloves, chopped very finely

450 g/1 lb pork sausage, peeled and chopped coarsely

3 canned pepperoncini, or other hot red peppers, drained and sliced

400 g/14 oz canned chopped tomatoes

2 tsp dried oregano

125 ml/4 fl oz chicken stock or red wine

salt and pepper

450 g/1 lb dried macaroni

12–15 black olives, stoned and quartered

75 g/2¾ oz freshly grated cheese, such as Cheddar or Gruyère cheese

Heat the oil in a large frying pan over a medium heat. Add the onion and fry for 5 minutes until soft. Add the garlic and fry for a few seconds until just beginning to colour. Add the sausage and fry until evenly browned.

Stir in the pepperoncini, tomatoes, oregano and stock. Season with salt and pepper. Bring to the boil, then simmer over a medium heat for 10 minutes, stirring occasionally.

Cook the macaroni in plenty of boiling salted water until al dente. Drain and transfer to a warm serving dish.

Add the olives and half the cheese to the sauce, then stir until the cheese has melted.

Pour the sauce over the pasta. Toss well to mix. Sprinkle with the remaining cheese and serve at once.

sausage & beef sauce
with peppers & tomatoes

ingredients

very easy   serves 4

15–20   1 hour
minutes   15 minutes

2 tbsp olive oil

4 bacon rashers, chopped

1 onion, chopped finely

1 green pepper, deseeded and chopped
   finely

50 g/1¾ oz mushrooms, sliced thinly

4 garlic cloves, sliced thinly

225 g/8 oz minced beef

225 g/8 oz coarse pork sausage, peeled
   and chopped

800 g/1 lb 12 oz canned chopped tomatoes

1 fresh bay leaf

6 tbsp tomato purée

4 tbsp red wine or stock

salt and pepper

450 g/1 lb dried penne or rigatoni

6 fresh basil leaves, shredded, to garnish

freshly grated Parmesan cheese, to serve

Heat the oil in a large frying pan over a medium heat. Add the bacon and fry until
lightly browned. Add the onion, green pepper, mushrooms and garlic. Gently fry
for 5–7 minutes until soft.

Stir in the beef and sausage, then cook until browned. Add the tomatoes and
bay leaf. Bring to the boil, then simmer over a medium–low heat for 1 hour.
Stir in the tomato purée and wine. Season with salt and pepper. Simmer for a
few minutes more.

Cook the pasta in plenty of boiling salted water until al dente. Drain and transfer
to a warm serving dish.

Pour the sauce over the pasta and toss well to mix. Sprinkle with the basil and
serve with Parmesan.

chicken & onion cream sauce

very easy

serves 4

10 minutes

35 minutes

ingredients

1 tbsp olive oil
2 tbsp butter
1 garlic clove, chopped very finely
4 boneless, skinless chicken breasts
salt and pepper
1 onion, chopped finely
1 chicken stock cube, crumbled
125 ml/4 fl oz water
300 ml/10 fl oz double cream

175 ml/6 fl oz milk
6 spring onions, green part included,
  sliced diagonally
35 g/1¼ oz freshly grated Parmesan cheese
450 g/1 lb dried fettuccine

chopped fresh flat-leaved parsley,
  to garnish

Heat the oil and butter with the garlic in a large frying pan over a medium–low heat. Cook the garlic until just beginning to colour. Add the chicken breasts and raise the heat to medium. Fry for 4–5 minutes on each side, until the juices are no longer pink. Season with salt and pepper. Remove from the heat. Remove the chicken breasts, leaving the oil in the pan. Slice the breasts diagonally into thin strips and set aside.

Reheat the oil in the pan. Add the onion and gently fry for 5 minutes until soft. Add the crumbled stock cube and the water. Bring to the boil, then simmer over a medium–low heat for 10 minutes. Stir in the cream, milk, spring onions and Parmesan. Simmer until heated through and slightly thickened.

Cook the fettucine in boiling salted water until al dente. Drain and transfer to a warm serving dish. Layer the chicken slices over the pasta. Pour on the sauce, garnish with parsley and serve.

cannelloni with chicken, ricotta & herbs

easy   serves 4

15–20 minutes + 30 minutes to marinate   1 hour

ingredients

MARINADE
125 ml/4 fl oz white wine vinegar
1 garlic clove, crushed
225 ml/8 fl oz olive oil

2 tbsp olive oil
4 boneless, skinless chicken breasts, diced
6 tbsp butter
500 ml/18 fl oz double cream
1 tsp salt

1 tsp freshly ground black pepper
¼ tsp freshly grated nutmeg
55 g/2 oz freshly grated Parmesan
450 g/1 lb ricotta cheese
1 egg, lightly beaten
1 tbsp chopped fresh oregano
2 tbsp chopped fresh basil
225 g/8 oz dried cannelloni
75 g/2¾ oz freshly grated mozzarella cheese

In a bowl, combine the vinegar, garlic and olive oil for the marinade. Add the chicken and marinate for 30 minutes.

Heat 2 tablespoons of olive oil in a frying pan. Drain the chicken and cook for 5–7 minutes, stirring, until no longer pink. Set aside.

Melt the butter in a saucepan over a medium–high heat. Add the cream, salt, pepper and nutmeg. Stir until thickened. Reduce the heat, add the Parmesan and stir until melted. Remove from the heat.

Heat the oven to 180°C/350°F/Gas Mark 4. In a large bowl, mix together the ricotta, egg and herbs. Stir in the chicken. Stuff the cannelloni with the chicken mixture. Pour half the sauce into a 23 x 33-cm/9 x 13-inch baking dish. Place the stuffed cannelloni on top. Pour over the remaining sauce. Sprinkle with the mozzarella and cover with aluminium foil. Bake for 45 minutes. Leave the dish to stand for 10 minutes before serving.

creamy chicken & shiitake sauce

very easy   serves 4

10 minutes   35 minutes
+ 30 minutes
soaking time

ingredients

25 g/1 oz dried shiitake mushrooms
350 ml/12 fl oz hot water
1 tbsp olive oil
6 bacon rashers, chopped
3 boneless, skinless chicken breasts, sliced
   into strips
115 g/4 oz fresh shiitake mushrooms,
   sliced
1 small onion, chopped finely

1 tsp fresh oregano or marjoram,
   chopped finely
250 ml/9 fl oz chicken stock
300 ml/10 fl oz whipping cream
salt and pepper
450 g/1 lb dried tagliatelle
55 g/2 oz freshly grated Parmesan cheese

chopped fresh flat-leaved parsley,
   to garnish

Put the dried mushrooms in a bowl with the hot water. Leave to soak for 30 minutes until softened. Remove, squeezing excess water back into the bowl. Strain the liquid in a fine-meshed sieve and reserve. Slice the soaked mushrooms, discarding the stems.

Heat the oil in a large frying pan over a medium heat. Add the bacon and chicken, then stir-fry for about 3 minutes. Add the dried and fresh mushrooms, the onion and oregano. Stir-fry for 5–7 minutes until soft. Pour in the stock and the mushroom liquid. Bring to the boil, stirring. Simmer briskly for about 10 minutes, continuing to stir, until reduced. Add the cream and simmer for 5 minutes, stirring, until beginning to thicken. Season with salt and pepper. Remove the pan from the heat and set aside.

Cook the pasta until al dente. Drain and transfer to a serving dish. Pour the sauce over the pasta. Add half the Parmesan and mix. Sprinkle with parsley and serve with the remaining Parmesan.

farfalle with chicken, broccoli & roasted red peppers

ingredients

very easy   serves 4

15 minutes   15 minutes

4 tbsp olive oil
5 tbsp butter
3 garlic cloves, chopped very finely
450 g/1 lb boneless, skinless chicken
    breasts, diced
¼ tsp dried chilli flakes
salt and pepper

450 g/1 lb small broccoli florets
300 g/10½ oz dried farfalle or fusilli
175 g/6 oz bottled roasted red peppers,
    drained and diced
250 ml/9 fl oz chicken stock

freshly grated Parmesan cheese, to serve

Bring a large pan of salted water to the boil. Meanwhile, heat the olive oil, butter and garlic in a large frying pan over a medium–low heat. Cook the garlic until just beginning to colour.

Add the diced chicken, raise the heat to medium and stir-fry for 4–5 minutes until the chicken is no longer pink. Add the chilli flakes and season with salt and pepper. Remove from the heat.

Plunge the broccoli into the boiling water and cook for 2 minutes until tender-crisp. Remove with a perforated spoon and set aside. Bring the water back to the boil. Add the pasta and cook until al dente. Drain and add to the chicken mixture in the pan. Add the broccoli and roasted peppers. Pour in the stock. Simmer briskly over a medium–high heat, stirring frequently, until most of the liquid has been absorbed.

Sprinkle with the Parmesan and serve.

chicken with basil & pine kernel pesto

very easy

serves 4

10 minutes   15 minutes

ingredients

PESTO
100 g/3½ oz shredded fresh basil
125 ml/4 fl oz extra-virgin olive oil
3 tbsp pine kernels
3 garlic cloves, crushed
salt
55 g/2 oz freshly grated Parmesan cheese

2 tbsp freshly grated pecorino cheese
2 tbsp vegetable oil
4 boneless, skinless chicken breasts
350 g/12 oz dried fettuccine
freshly ground pepper to taste

sprig of fresh basil, to garnish

To make the pesto, put the basil, olive oil, pine kernels, garlic and a generous pinch of salt in a food processor or blender. Purée the ingredients until smooth. Scrape the mixture into a bowl and stir in the cheeses.

Heat the vegetable oil in a frying pan over a medium heat. Fry the chicken breasts, turning once, for 8–10 minutes until the juices are no longer pink. Cut into small cubes.

Cook the pasta in plenty of boiling salted water until al dente. Drain and transfer to a warm serving dish. Add the chicken and pesto, then season with pepper. Toss well to mix.

Garnish with a sprig of basil and serve warm.

noodles with chicken satay sauce

very easy

serves 4

10 minutes   20 minutes

ingredients

2 tbsp vegetable oil
450 g/1 lb boneless, skinless chicken
  breasts, cubed
1 red pepper, deseeded and sliced
4 spring onions, green part included, sliced
  diagonally

225 g/8 oz dried vermicelli or spaghettini
125 g/4½ oz smooth peanut butter
1 tsp grated fresh ginger root
2 tbsp soy sauce
125 ml/4 fl oz chicken stock

Heat the oil in a large frying pan over a medium heat. Add the chicken and fry for 5–7 minutes until no longer pink. Add the pepper and spring onions. Fry for 3 minutes until just soft. Remove from the heat.

Cook the pasta in plenty of boiling salted water until al dente. Drain and return to the pan.

Put the peanut butter, ginger, soy sauce and chicken stock in a large saucepan. Simmer over a medium–low heat, stirring, until bubbling. Add the cooked vegetables, chicken and pasta to the peanut mixture. Toss gently until coated with the sauce.

Transfer to a warm serving dish and serve immediately.

fusilli with bacon, eggs & mushrooms

very easy

serves 4

10 minutes   15 minutes

ingredients

1 tbsp olive oil
4 rashers streaky bacon or pancetta
115 g/4 oz mushrooms, sliced
225 g/8 oz fusilli or conchiglie
salt and pepper

2 eggs, beaten
115 g/4 oz Cheddar or mozzarella cheese,
    cubed

chopped fresh flat-leaved parsley,
    to garnish

Heat the oil in a frying pan over a medium heat. Add the bacon and fry until crisp. Remove with tongs, leaving the drippings in the pan. Cut into small pieces and keep warm.

Fry the mushrooms in the bacon drippings for 5–7 minutes until soft. Remove from the heat.

Cook the pasta in plenty of boiling salted water until al dente. Drain and return to the pan.

Stir the mushrooms, beaten eggs and the cheese cubes into the pasta. Season with pepper and toss until the eggs have coated the pasta and the cheese has melted.

Transfer to a warm serving dish. Sprinkle with the bacon pieces and parsley and serve at once.

rigatoni with spicy bacon & tomato sauce

very easy   serves 4

10 minutes   45 minutes

ingredients

6 tbsp olive oil

3 garlic cloves, sliced thinly

75 g/2¾ oz streaky bacon, chopped

800 g/1 lb 12 oz canned chopped tomatoes

½ tsp dried chilli flakes

salt and pepper

450 g/1 lb rigatoni

10 fresh basil leaves, shredded

2 tbsp freshly grated pecorino cheese

Heat the oil and garlic in a large frying pan over a medium–low heat. Cook until the garlic is just beginning to colour. Add the bacon and cook until browned.

Stir in the tomatoes and chilli flakes. Season with a little salt and pepper. Bring to the boil, then simmer over a medium–low heat for 30–40 minutes, until the oil separates from the tomatoes.

Cook the pasta in plenty of boiling salted water until al dente. Drain and transfer to a warm serving dish.

Pour the sauce over the pasta. Add the basil and pecorino, then toss well to mix. Serve at once.

ham, tomato & chilli sauce

very easy · serves 4

10–15 minutes · 1 hour

ingredients

1 tbsp olive oil
2 tbsp butter
1 onion, chopped finely
150 g/5½ oz ham, diced
2 garlic cloves, chopped very finely
1 fresh red chilli, deseeded and chopped
  finely

800 g/1 lb 12 oz canned chopped tomatoes
salt and pepper
450 g/1 lb bucatini or penne
2 tbsp chopped fresh flat-leaved parsley
6 tbsp freshly grated Parmesan cheese

Put the olive oil and 1 tablespoon of the butter in a large saucepan over a medium–low heat. Add the onion and fry for 10 minutes until soft and golden. Add the ham and fry for 5 minutes until lightly browned. Stir in the garlic, chilli and tomatoes. Season with a little salt and pepper. Bring to the boil, then simmer over a medium–low heat for 30–40 minutes until thickened.

Cook the pasta in plenty of boiling salted water until al dente. Drain and transfer to a warm serving dish.

Pour the sauce over the pasta. Add the parsley, Parmesan and the remaining butter. Toss well to mix. Serve immediately.

spaghetti alla carbonara

very easy   serves 4

10–15
minutes   15 minutes

ingredients

2 tbsp olive oil

1 tbsp butter

175 g/6 oz smoked streaky bacon,
    sliced into thin strips

3 eggs, lightly beaten

35 g/1¼ oz freshly grated Parmesan cheese

20 g/¾ oz freshly grated pecorino cheese

1 tbsp chopped fresh flat-leaved parsley

4 tbsp single cream

pepper

450 g/1 lb dried spaghetti, chopped

Heat the oil and butter in a frying pan over a medium–high heat. Add the bacon and fry for 4–5 minutes until browned. Remove from the heat. Combine the eggs, cheeses, parsley and cream in a bowl, mixing well. Season with pepper.

Cook the pasta in plenty of boiling salted water until al dente. Drain and return to the pan.

Quickly add the egg mixture to the pasta, tossing rapidly so that the egg cooks in the heat. Transfer to a warm serving dish.

Briefly reheat the bacon over a high heat. Add to the pasta, toss again and serve at once.

With their flamboyant colours and fresh flavours, Mediterranean-style vegetables and herbs are perfect for pasta sauces. These are among the quickest and easiest sauces to prepare, ranging from the simple concoctions of chopped raw tomatoes, olive oil and basil to more complex mixtures of roasted peppers and garlic, or asparagus and Gorgonzola. Storecupboard ingredients are put to good use: jars of artichokes, peppers, sun-dried tomatoes and olives all contribute robust flavours that will please vegetarians and meat-eaters alike.

vegetable sauces

sun-dried tomato & goat's cheese sauce

very easy   serves 4

10 minutes   10–15
minutes

ingredients

1 tbsp butter
2 garlic cloves, sliced thinly
225 g/8 oz goat's cheese, crumbled
300 ml/10 fl oz milk
150 ml/5 fl oz double cream
20 oil-cured sun-dried tomato halves
  (in oil), chopped roughly

salt and pepper
450 g/1 lb dried penne
35 g/1¼ oz freshly grated Parmesan cheese
10 fresh basil leaves, shredded

Heat the butter and garlic in a frying pan over a medium–low heat. Cook until the garlic is just beginning to colour. Add the cheese and milk. Stir until the cheese has melted and formed a thick sauce.

Add the cream and sun-dried tomatoes. Cook for about 5 minutes, stirring frequently, until reduced by one-third. Season with salt and pepper. Remove from the heat.

Cook the pasta in plenty of boiling salted water until al dente. Transfer to a warm serving dish.

Briefly reheat the sauce over a low heat. Pour over the pasta. Add the Parmesan and basil, then toss well to mix. Serve immediately.

sun-dried tomato sauce with herbs

very easy　　serves 4

10–15
minutes

20–25
minutes

ingredients

85 g/3 oz sun-dried tomatoes (not in oil)

700 ml/1¼ pints boiling water

2 tbsp olive oil

1 onion, chopped finely

2 large garlic cloves, sliced finely

2 tbsp chopped fresh flat-leaved parsley

2 tsp chopped fresh oregano

1 tsp chopped fresh rosemary

salt and pepper

350 g/12 oz dried fusilli

10 fresh basil leaves, shredded

3 tbsp freshly grated Parmesan cheese

Put the tomatoes and boiling water in a bowl and leave to stand for 5 minutes. Using a perforated spoon, remove one-third of the tomatoes from the bowl. Cut into bite-sized pieces. Put the remaining tomatoes and water into a blender and purée.

Heat the oil in a large frying pan over a medium heat. Add the onion and gently fry for 5 minutes until soft. Add the garlic and fry until just beginning to colour. Add the puréed tomato and the reserved tomato pieces to the pan. Bring to the boil, then simmer over a medium–low heat for 10 minutes. Stir in the herbs and season with salt and pepper. Simmer for 1 minute, then remove from the heat.

Cook the pasta in plenty of boiling salted water until al dente. Drain and transfer to a warm serving dish. Briefly reheat the sauce. Pour over the pasta, add the basil and toss well to mix. Sprinkle with the Parmesan and serve immediately.

tomato-chilli sauce with avocado & coriander

very easy   serves 4

15 minutes   20 minutes

ingredients

3 tbsp olive oil

4 spring onions, green part included, sliced finely

1 fresh green chilli, deseeded and chopped very finely

2 garlic cloves, chopped very finely

200 g/7 oz canned chopped tomatoes

salt and pepper

350 g/12 oz dried farfalle or conchiglie

2 small avocados, peeled and cubed

juice of ½ lime

6 tbsp chopped fresh coriander

Heat 1 tablespoon of the oil in a frying pan over a medium–low heat. Add the spring onions and chilli, then fry, stirring constantly, for 3–4 minutes until just soft. Add the garlic and fry until just beginning to colour.

Stir in the tomatoes. Bring to the boil, then simmer the sauce over a medium heat for 10 minutes, stirring, until thickened. Season with salt and pepper.

Cook the pasta in plenty of boiling salted water until al dente. Drain and transfer to a warm serving dish.

Pour the sauce over the pasta. Add the avocados, lime juice, coriander and remaining olive oil. Toss well to mix. Serve warm or at room temperature.

pepper & goat's cheese sauce

very easy   serves 4

10 minutes   30 minutes

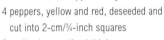

ingredients

2 tbsp olive oil

1 tbsp butter

1 small onion, chopped finely

4 peppers, yellow and red, deseeded and
    cut into 2-cm/¾-inch squares

3 garlic cloves, sliced thinly

salt and pepper

450 g/1 lb dried rigatoni or penne

125 g/4½ oz goat's cheese, crumbled

15 fresh basil leaves, shredded

10 black olives, stoned and sliced

Heat the oil and butter in a large frying pan over a medium heat. Add the onion
and fry until soft. Raise the heat to medium–high and add the peppers and garlic.
Cook for 12–15 minutes, stirring, until the peppers are tender but not mushy.
Season with salt and pepper. Remove from the heat.

Cook the pasta in plenty of boiling salted water until al dente. Drain and transfer
to a warm serving dish. Add the goat's cheese and toss to mix.

Briefly reheat the sauce. Add the basil and olives. Pour over the pasta and toss
well to mix. Serve immediately.

tomato sauce with garlic & basil

very easy   serves 4

10 minutes   30 minutes

ingredients

5 tbsp extra-virgin olive oil

1 onion, chopped finely

800 g/1 lb 12 oz canned chopped tomatoes

4 garlic cloves, quartered

salt and pepper

450 g/1 lb dried spaghetti

large handful fresh basil leaves, shredded

freshly grated Parmesan cheese, to serve

Heat the oil in a large saucepan over a medium heat. Add the onion and fry gently for 5 minutes until soft. Add the tomatoes and garlic. Bring to the boil, then simmer over a medium–low heat for 25–30 minutes until the oil separates from the tomato. Season with salt and pepper.

Cook the pasta in plenty of boiling salted water until al dente. Drain and transfer to a warm serving dish.

Pour the sauce over the pasta. Add the basil and toss well to mix. Serve with Parmesan.

raw tomato sauce with olive oil, garlic & basil

extremely
easy

serves 4

10 minutes
+ 30 minutes
standing
time

8–10
minutes

ingredients

550 g/1 lb 4 oz large, ripe tomatoes,
   peeled, deseeded and diced
125 ml/4 fl oz extra-virgin olive oil
4 garlic cloves, chopped very finely

large handful fresh basil leaves, shredded
3 tbsp chopped fresh oregano or marjoram
salt and pepper
450 g/1 lb dried conchiglie

Combine the tomatoes, olive oil, garlic, basil and oregano in a bowl that is large
enough eventually to accommodate the cooked pasta. Season generously with salt
and pepper. Cover the bowl with clingfilm and leave to stand at room temperature
for at least 30 minutes.

Cook the pasta in plenty of boiling salted water until al dente. Drain thoroughly
and immediately add to the tomatoes.

Toss well to mix. Serve at room temperature.

cherry tomato sauce with olives

ingredients

very easy   serves 4

10 minutes   30 minutes

4 tbsp olive oil
900 g/2 lb cherry tomatoes
2 garlic cloves, chopped very finely
1 tbsp chopped fresh oregano or marjoram
¼ tsp dried chilli flakes

20–25 black olives, stoned and sliced
pepper
350 g/12 oz dried conchiglie
rind of ½ lemon, grated
20 g/¾ oz freshly grated Parmesan cheese

Heat the oil in a large frying pan over a medium–high heat. Add the cherry tomatoes and stir until evenly coated with oil. Cover and cook for 10–12 minutes, shaking the pan and stirring once, until all the tomatoes have split.

Add the garlic, oregano, chilli flakes and olives. Season with pepper. Reduce the heat to low and simmer, uncovered, for another 7–10 minutes.

Cook the pasta in plenty of boiling salted water until al dente. Drain well and transfer to a warm serving dish.

Pour half the sauce over the pasta. Toss well to mix. Spoon the rest of the sauce over the top. Sprinkle with the grated lemon rind and Parmesan and serve at once.

roasted red pepper sauce

very easy   serves 4

10 minutes   35 minutes

ingredients

4 red peppers, halved and deseeded
5 tbsp olive oil
1 small red onion, sliced finely
2 garlic cloves, chopped very finely
2 tbsp chopped fresh flat-leaved parsley
1 tsp chopped fresh thyme
salt and pepper

350 g/12 oz dried penne or rigatoni

4 tbsp toasted fresh breadcrumbs,
  to garnish

freshly grated Parmesan cheese, to serve

Place the peppers cut side down in a roasting tin. Roast in a preheated oven at 220°C/425°F/Gas Mark 7 for 15–20 minutes until the skin begins to blacken. Leave to cool slightly. Remove the skin from the peppers. Slice the flesh into thin strips.

Heat the oil in a large frying pan over a medium heat. Add the onion and fry for 5 minutes until soft. Add the garlic and fry until just beginning to colour. Stir in the roasted pepper strips, parsley and thyme. Season with salt and pepper. Stir until heated through.

Cook the pasta in plenty of boiling salted water until al dente. Drain well and transfer to a warm serving dish.

Pour the sauce over the pasta and toss well to mix. Sprinkle with the breadcrumbs and serve with Parmesan.

roasted garlic & red pepper sauce

very easy   serves 4

10 minutes   30 minutes

ingredients

6 large garlic cloves, unpeeled
400 g/14 oz bottled roasted red peppers,
    drained and sliced
200 g/7 oz canned chopped tomatoes
3 tbsp olive oil
¼ tsp dried chilli flakes

1 tsp chopped fresh thyme or oregano
salt and pepper
350 g/12 oz dried spaghetti, bucatini
    or linguine

freshly grated Parmesan cheese, to serve

Place the unpeeled garlic cloves in a shallow, ovenproof dish. Roast in a preheated oven at 200°C/400°F/Gas Mark 6 for 7–10 minutes until the cloves feel soft.

Put the peppers, tomatoes and oil in a food processor or blender, then purée. Squeeze the garlic flesh into the purée. Add the chilli flakes and oregano. Season with salt and pepper. Blend again, then scrape into a saucepan and set aside.

Cook the pasta in plenty of boiling salted water until al dente. Drain and transfer to a warm serving dish.

Reheat the sauce and pour over the pasta. Toss well to mix. Serve at once with Parmesan.

marinated artichoke sauce with onions & tomatoes

ingredients

very easy   serves 4

10 minutes   50 minutes

280 g/10 oz marinated artichoke hearts
(in jar)
3 tbsp olive oil
1 onion, chopped finely
3 garlic cloves, chopped very finely
1 tsp dried oregano

¼ tsp dried chilli flakes
400 g/14 oz canned chopped tomatoes
salt and pepper
350 g/12 oz dried conchiglie
20 g/¾ oz freshly grated Parmesan cheese
3 tbsp chopped fresh flat-leaved parsley

Drain the artichoke hearts, reserving the marinade. Heat the oil in a large saucepan over a medium heat. Add the onion and fry for 5 minutes until translucent. Add the garlic, oregano, chilli flakes and the reserved artichoke marinade. Cook for 5 more minutes.

Stir in the tomatoes. Bring to the boil, then simmer over a medium–low heat for 30 minutes. Season generously with salt and pepper.

Cook the pasta in plenty of boiling salted water until al dente. Drain and transfer to a warm serving dish.

Add the artichokes, Parmesan and parsley to the sauce. Cook for a few minutes until heated through.

Pour the sauce over the pasta. Toss well to mix. Serve at once.

asparagus & gorgonzola sauce with cream

extremely easy   serves 4

10 minutes   20 minutes

ingredients

450 g/1 lb asparagus tips
olive oil
salt and pepper

225 g/8 oz Gorgonzola cheese, crumbled
175 ml/6 fl oz double cream
350 g/12 oz dried penne

Place the asparagus tips in a single layer in a shallow ovenproof dish. Sprinkle with a little olive oil. Season with salt and pepper. Turn to coat in the oil and seasoning.

Roast in a preheated oven at 230°C/450°F/Gas Mark 8 for 10–12 minutes until slightly browned and just tender. Set aside and keep warm.

Combine the crumbled cheese with the cream in a bowl. Season with salt and pepper.

Cook the pasta in plenty of boiling salted water until al dente. Drain and transfer to a warm serving dish.

Immediately add the asparagus and the cheese mixture. Toss well until the cheese has melted and the pasta is coated with the sauce. Serve at once.

spaghetti with garlic & oil sauce

extremely easy   serves 4

10 minutes   25 minutes

ingredients

450 g/1 lb dried spaghetti
salt
125 ml/4 fl oz extra-virgin olive oil

4 garlic cloves, chopped very finely
¼ tsp dried chilli flakes
3 tbsp chopped fresh flat-leaved parsley

Cook the pasta in plenty of boiling salted water until al dente. Drain and transfer to a warm serving dish. Season with salt to taste and keep the dish warm.

Heat the oil in a small saucepan over a medium–low heat. Add the garlic and chilli flakes. Cook for 1–2 minutes until the garlic is just beginning to colour. Immediately pour the contents of the saucepan over the pasta. Toss thoroughly to mix.

Sprinkle with the parsley and toss again. Serve immediately.

roasted garlic cream sauce

easy

serves 4

10 minutes   20 minutes

ingredients

2 large heads garlic
600 ml/1 pint double cream
3 thin strips lemon peel
salt and pepper

350 g/12 oz dried fettuccine or tagliatelle
35 g/1¼ oz freshly grated Parmesan cheese

2 tbsp chopped fresh flat-leaved parsley,
   to garnish

Separate the garlic cloves, removing as much of the papery skin as possible, but leaving a thin layer intact. Place the cloves in a shallow ovenproof dish. Roast in a preheated oven at 200°C/400°F/ Gas Mark 6 for 7–10 minutes until the cloves feel soft.

When the garlic is cool enough to handle, remove the skin. Put the cloves in a small saucepan with the cream and lemon peel. Bring to the boil, then simmer gently over a low heat for about 5 minutes until thickened. Push the sauce through a fine-meshed sieve, pressing with the back of a wooden spoon. Return to the saucepan. Season with salt and pepper and set aside.

Cook the pasta in plenty of boiling salted water until al dente. Drain and transfer to a warm serving dish. Stir the Parmesan into the sauce and reheat gently. Pour the sauce over the pasta and toss well to mix. Sprinkle with the parsley. Serve immediately.

mushroom & spinach sauce with feta

very easy   serves 4

15 minutes   20 minutes

ingredients

3 tbsp olive oil
225 g/8 oz mushrooms, sliced
2 garlic cloves, chopped very finely
2 tbsp chopped fresh flat-leaved parsley
salt and pepper
450 g/1 lb dried rigatoni
250 g/9 oz trimmed baby spinach,
   chopped roughly
250 ml/9 fl oz hot chicken stock

TO GARNISH
55 g/2 oz feta cheese (drained
   weight), crumbled
1 tsp chopped fresh thyme

Heat the oil in a large frying pan over a medium–high heat. Add the mushrooms and fry for 5 minutes until the moisture starts to evaporate. Add the garlic and parsley, then cook for a few seconds more. Season with salt and pepper. Remove the cooking pan from the heat.

Cook the pasta in plenty of boiling salted water until al dente. Drain and immediately return to the pan.

Add the spinach, hot stock and the mushrooms to the pasta. Toss well until the spinach has wilted. Transfer to a warm serving dish. Sprinkle with the feta and thyme and serve at once.

courgette sauce with lemon & rosemary

very easy   serves 4

10 minutes   20 minutes

ingredients

6 tbsp olive oil

1 small onion, sliced very thinly

2 garlic cloves, chopped very finely

2 tbsp chopped fresh rosemary

1 tbsp chopped fresh flat-leaved parsley

450 g/1 lb small courgettes,
   cut into 4 cm x 5-mm/1½ x ¼-inch strips

finely grated peel of 1 lemon

salt and pepper

450 g/1 lb fusilli

4 tbsp freshly grated Parmesan cheese

Heat the olive oil in a large frying pan over a medium–low heat. Add the onion and gently fry, stirring occasionally, for about 10 minutes until golden.

Raise the heat to medium–high. Add the garlic, rosemary and parsley. Cook for a few seconds, stirring.

Add the courgettes and lemon peel. Cook for 5–7 minutes, stirring occasionally, until the courgettes are just tender. Season with salt and pepper. Remove from the heat.

Cook the pasta in plenty of boiling salted water until al dente. Drain and transfer to a warm serving dish.

Briefly reheat the courgettes. Pour over the pasta and toss well to mix. Sprinkle with the Parmesan and serve immediately.

Fish and seafood are ideal candidates for pasta sauces, especially if you stock up with storecupboard basics such as bottled clams and cans of tuna and anchovies. These need only the briefest of cooking times, allowing you to get a meal on the table in minutes. Prawns can be combined with tomatoes, garlic and chilli for a robust Mediterranean sauce, or sizzled oriental-style with ginger and spices, while smoked salmon, mussels and scallops can form the basis of rich cream or tomato-based sauces that are ideal for entertaining.

fish & seafood
sauces

spaghetti with anchovies, olives, capers & tomatoes

very easy   serves 4

10 minutes   35–40
minutes

ingredients

6 tbsp olive oil

4 anchovy fillets, chopped

2 garlic cloves, chopped very finely

800 g/1 lb 12 oz canned chopped tomatoes

1 tsp dried oregano

¼ tsp dried chilli flakes

salt and pepper

350 g/12 oz dried spaghetti

10–12 black olives, stoned and sliced

2 tbsp capers, drained

Heat the oil with the anchovies in a large frying pan over a low heat. Stir until the anchovies dissolve. Add the garlic and cook for a few seconds until just beginning to colour. Add the tomatoes, oregano and chilli flakes, then season with salt and pepper. Bring to the boil, then simmer over a medium–low heat for 30 minutes until the oil begins to separate from the tomatoes.

Cook the pasta in plenty of boiling salted water until al dente. Drain and transfer to a warm serving dish.

Add the olives and capers to the sauce. Pour over the pasta and toss well to mix. Serve immediately.

clam & tomato sauce

very easy   serves 4

10 minutes   35 minutes

ingredients

400 g/14 oz clams or scallops in brine
(in jar)
4 tbsp olive oil
4 garlic cloves, chopped very finely
800 g/1 lb 12 oz canned chopped tomatoes

3 tbsp chopped fresh flat-leaved parsley
½ tsp dried chilli flakes
salt
450 g/1 lb dried riccioli or fusilli

Drain the clams or scallops, reserving the liquid from the jar.

Heat the oil and garlic in a large saucepan over a low heat. Cook the garlic for
a few seconds until just beginning to colour. Add the tomatoes, the reserved
clam juice, parsley, chilli flakes and a little salt. Bring to the boil, then simmer
over a medium–low heat for 30 minutes until the oil separates from the tomatoes.

Cook the pasta in plenty of boiling salted water until al dente. Drain and transfer
to a warm serving dish.

Add the clams to the sauce, stirring until heated through. Pour the sauce over the
pasta. Toss well to mix. Serve immediately.

prawn sauce with tomatoes, garlic & chilli

very easy   serves 4

10 minutes   35 minutes

ingredients

4 tbsp olive oil
5 garlic cloves, chopped very finely
400 g/14 oz canned chopped tomatoes
1 fresh red chilli, deseeded and chopped
  very finely
salt and pepper

450 g/1 lb dried linguine or spaghetti
350 g/12 oz raw peeled prawns

2 tbsp chopped fresh flat-leaved parsley,
  to garnish

Heat 2 tablespoons of the oil and the garlic in a saucepan over a medium–low heat. Cook the garlic until just beginning to colour. Add the tomatoes and chilli. Bring to the boil, then simmer over a medium–low heat for 30 minutes until the oil separates from the tomatoes. Season with salt and pepper.

Cook the pasta in plenty of boiling salted water until al dente. Drain and return to the pan.

Heat the remaining oil in a frying pan over a high heat. Add the prawns and stir-fry for 2 minutes until pink. Add the prawns to the tomato mixture. Stir in the parsley. Simmer over a low heat until bubbling.

Transfer the pasta to a warm serving dish. Pour the sauce over the pasta. Toss well to mix and serve immediately.

clam & leek sauce

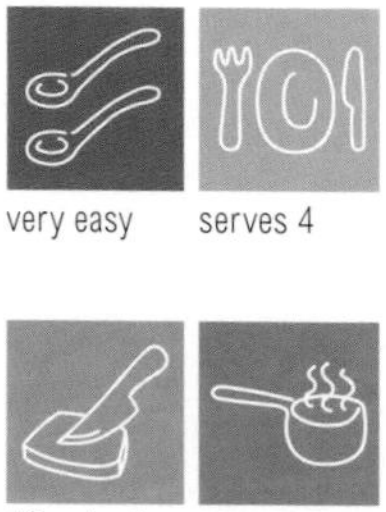

very easy serves 4

10 minutes 15 minutes

ingredients

400 g/14 oz clams in brine (in jar)
3 tbsp olive oil
2 large leeks (white part only), sliced lengthwise and cut into thin 5-cm/2-inch strips
2 garlic cloves, chopped very finely
4 tbsp dry white wine
1 bay leaf
salt and pepper
350 g/12 oz dried spaghetti or linguine
3 tbsp fresh flat-leaved parsley

Drain the clams, reserving the liquid from the jar.

Heat the oil in a large frying pan over a medium–low heat. Add the leeks and garlic, then fry gently for 3–4 minutes until the leeks are tender-crisp. Stir in the wine and cook for 1–2 minutes until evaporated. Add the bay leaf, clams and the reserved liquid. Season with salt and pepper. Simmer for 5 minutes, then remove from the heat.

Cook the pasta in plenty of boiling salted water until al dente. Drain and transfer to a warm serving dish.

Briefly reheat the sauce and pour over the pasta. Add the parsley and toss well to mix. Serve immediately.

prawn & garlic sauce with cream

very easy   serves 4

15 minutes   15 minutes

ingredients

3 tbsp olive oil
3 tbsp butter
4 garlic cloves, chopped very finely
2 tbsp finely diced red pepper
2 tbsp tomato purée
125 ml/4 fl oz dry white wine

450 g/1 lb tagliatelle or spaghetti
350 g/12 oz raw peeled prawns, cut into
  1-cm/½-inch pieces
125 ml/4 fl oz double cream
salt and pepper
3 tbsp chopped fresh flat-leaved parsley

Heat the oil and butter in a saucepan over a medium–low heat. Add the garlic and red pepper. Fry for a few seconds until the garlic is just beginning to colour. Stir in the tomato purée and wine. Cook for 10 minutes, stirring.

Cook the pasta in plenty of boiling salted water until al dente. Drain and return to the pan.

Add the prawns to the sauce and raise the heat to medium–high. Cook for 2 minutes, stirring, until the prawns turn pink. Reduce the heat and stir in the cream. Cook for 1 minute, stirring constantly, until thickened. Season with salt and pepper.

Transfer the pasta to a warm serving dish. Pour the sauce over the pasta. Sprinkle with the parsley. Toss well to mix and serve at once.

spicy prawn sauce with ginger

very easy   serves 4

10 minutes   10 minutes

ingredients

4 tbsp passata (sieved tomatoes)
300 ml/10 fl oz single cream
1½ tsp grated fresh ginger
¼ tsp cayenne
1 tbsp lemon juice
1 tsp ground cumin
1 tsp salt

¼ tsp pepper
450 g/1 lb dried flat rice noodles
3 tbsp vegetable oil
3 garlic cloves, chopped very finely
450 g/1 lb raw peeled prawns
2 tbsp chopped fresh coriander

Combine the passata, cream, ginger, cayenne, lemon juice, cumin, salt and pepper in a small saucepan, mixing well. Cook the mixture over a medium heat, stirring, until bubbling. Remove from the heat.

Cook the noodles according to the packet instructions. Drain and transfer to a warm serving dish.

Heat the oil and garlic in a large frying pan over a medium—low heat. Cook until the garlic just begins to colour. Add the prawns and raise the heat to medium—high. Stir-fry for 2 minutes until the prawns are pink. Stir in the sauce and 1 tablespoon of the coriander. Cook for another minute.

Pour the prawn mixture over the noodles. Sprinkle with the remaining coriander and serve immediately.

prawn sauce with lemon & herbs

very easy   serves 4

15–20 minutes   10 minutes

ingredients

350 g/12 oz dried spaghettini or vermicelli
4 tbsp olive oil
4 tbsp butter
8 spring onions, green part included,
   sliced thinly
450 g/1 lb raw peeled prawns
juice and finely grated peel of ½ lemon

3 tbsp chopped fresh flat-leaved parsley
3 tbsp shredded fresh basil
1 tbsp chopped fresh marjoram or oregano
2 tsp chopped fresh thyme
250 ml/9 fl oz chicken stock
salt and pepper

Cook the pasta in plenty of boiling salted water until al dente. Drain and return to the pan and cover to keep warm.

Heat the oil and butter in a large frying pan over a medium–high heat. Add the spring onions and prawns. Stir-fry for 2 minutes until the prawns turn pink. Reduce the heat to medium. Stir in the lemon juice and peel, herbs and chicken stock. Season with salt and pepper. Simmer until heated through.

Transfer the pasta to a warm serving dish. Pour the prawn mixture over the pasta and toss well to mix. Serve immediately.

scallops with porcini & cream sauce

very easy   serves 4

10 minutes + 25 minutes
20 minutes
soaking time

ingredients

25 g/1 oz dried porcini mushrooms
500 ml/18 fl oz hot water
3 tbsp olive oil
3 tbsp butter
350 g/12 oz scallops, sliced
2 garlic cloves, chopped very finely

2 tbsp lemon juice
250 ml/9 fl oz double cream
salt and pepper
350 g/12 oz dried fettuccine or pappardelle
2 tbsp chopped fresh flat-leaved parsley

Put the porcini and hot water in a bowl. Leave to soak for 20 minutes. Strain the mushrooms, reserving the soaking water, and chop roughly. Line a sieve with two pieces of kitchen paper and strain the mushroom water into a bowl.

Heat the oil and butter in a large frying pan over a medium heat. Add the scallops and cook for 2 minutes until just golden. Add the garlic and mushrooms, then stir-fry for another minute.

Stir in the lemon juice, cream and 125 ml/4 fl oz of the mushroom water. Bring to the boil, then simmer over a medium heat for 2–3 minutes, stirring constantly, until the liquid is reduced by half. Season with salt and pepper. Remove from the heat.

Cook the pasta in plenty of boiling salted water until al dente. Drain and transfer to a warm serving dish. Briefly reheat the sauce and pour over the pasta. Sprinkle with the parsley and toss well to mix. Serve immediately.

tuna with garlic, lemon, capers & olives

extremely easy

serves 4

10 minutes

10 minutes

ingredients

350 g/12 oz dried conchiglie or gnocchi

4 tbsp olive oil

4 tbsp butter

3 large garlic cloves, sliced thinly

200 g/7 oz canned tuna, drained and broken
  into chunks

2 tbsp lemon juice

1 tbsp capers, drained

10–12 black olives, stoned and sliced

2 tbsp chopped fresh flat-leaved parsley

Cook the pasta in plenty of boiling salted water until al dente. Drain and return to the pan.

Heat the olive oil and half the butter in a frying pan over a medium–low heat. Add the garlic and cook for a few seconds until just beginning to colour. Reduce the heat to low. Add the tuna, lemon juice, capers and olives. Stir gently until all the ingredients are heated through.

Transfer the pasta to a warm serving dish. Pour the tuna mixture over the pasta. Add the parsley and remaining butter. Toss well to mix. Serve immediately.

mussels with tomatoes, peppers & olives

ingredients

very easy   serves 4

20 minutes   20 minutes

3 litres/5¼ pints mussels	400 g/14 oz canned chopped tomatoes
1 large onion, chopped finely	¼ tsp dried chilli flakes
250 ml/9 fl oz dry white wine	salt and pepper
3 tbsp olive oil	450 g/1 lb riccioli or fettucine
3 garlic cloves, chopped very finely	10–12 black olives, stoned and sliced
2 yellow peppers, deseeded and diced	6 tbsp shredded fresh basil

Clean the mussels by scrubbing the shells and pulling out any beards that are attached. Rinse well and discard any with broken shells and any that do not close when tapped. Put the mussels in a large saucepan with the onion and white wine. Cover and cook over a medium heat for 3–4 minutes, shaking the pan, until the mussels open. Remove from the heat. Lift out the mussels with a perforated spoon, reserving the liquid. Discard any that remain closed. Remove the rest of the mussels from their shells.

Heat the olive oil and garlic in a frying pan over a medium–low heat. Cook until the garlic is just beginning to colour. Add the peppers, tomatoes, chilli flakes and 4 tablespoons of the mussel liquid. Bring to the boil, then simmer over a medium heat for 15 minutes until slightly reduced. Season with salt and pepper. Cook the pasta until al dente. Drain and transfer to a serving dish. Add the mussels and olives to the sauce; stir until heated. Pour onto the pasta. Add the basil and mix well. Serve at once.

mussels with white wine, garlic & parsley

very easy   serves 4

20 minutes   10 minutes

ingredients

3.5 litres/6 pints mussels, scrubbed

1 large onion, chopped

3 garlic cloves, chopped very finely

500 ml/18 fl oz dry white wine

1 bay leaf

2 sprigs of fresh thyme

5 tbsp chopped fresh flat-leaved parsley

1 tbsp chopped fresh rosemary

4 tbsp butter

salt and pepper

450 g/1 lb dried tagliatelle or other broad-
 ribboned pasta

Clean the mussels by scrubbing the shells and pulling out any beards that are attached. Rinse well, discarding any with broken shells or that remain open when tapped. Put the onion, garlic, white wine, herbs and 2 tablespoons of the butter in a saucepan. Bring to the boil, then reduce the heat. Add the mussels. Season to taste. Cover and cook over a medium heat for 3–4 minutes, shaking the pan, until the mussels open. Remove from the heat. Lift out the mussels with a perforated spoon, reserving the liquid. Discard any that remain closed. Remove most of the others from their shells, reserving a few in their shells to garnish.

Cook the pasta until al dente. Drain and put the pasta into bowls. Spoon the mussels over the pasta. Strain the mussel liquid and return to the pan. Add the remaining butter and heat until melted. Pour over the pasta, garnish with the mussels in their shells and serve immediately.

smoked salmon, soured cream & mustard sauce

ingredients

extremely easy

serves 4

10 minutes

10 minutes

450 g/1 lb tagliatelle or conchiglie
300 ml/10 fl oz soured cream
2 tsp Dijon mustard
4 large spring onions, sliced finely
225 g/8 oz smoked salmon, cut into
   bite-sized pieces

finely grated peel of ½ lemon
pepper

2 tbsp chopped fresh chives, to garnish

Cook the pasta in plenty of boiling salted water until al dente. Drain and return to the pan. Add the soured cream, mustard, spring onions, smoked salmon and lemon peel to the pasta. Stir over a low heat until heated through. Season with pepper.

Transfer to a serving dish. Sprinkle with the chives. Serve warm or at room temperature.

hot cajun seafood sauce

very easy   serves 4

15 minutes   20 minutes

ingredients

500 ml/18 fl oz whipping cream
8 spring onions, sliced thinly
55 g/2 oz chopped fresh flat-leaved parsley
1 tbsp chopped fresh thyme
½ tbsp freshly ground black pepper
½–1 tsp dried chilli flakes
1 tsp salt
450 g/1 lb dried fusilli or tagliatelle

40 g/1½ oz freshly grated Gruyère cheese
20 g/¾ oz freshly grated Parmesan cheese
2 tbsp olive oil
225 g/8 oz raw peeled prawns
225 g/8 oz scallops, sliced

1 tbsp shredded fresh basil, to garnish

Heat the cream in a large saucepan over a medium heat, stirring constantly. When almost boiling, reduce the heat and add the spring onions, parsley, thyme, pepper, chilli flakes and salt. Simmer for 7–8 minutes, stirring, until thickened. Remove from the heat.

Cook the pasta in plenty of boiling salted water until al dente. Drain and return to the pan. Add the cream mixture and the cheeses to the pasta. Toss over a low heat until the cheeses have melted. Transfer to a warm serving dish.

Heat the oil in a large frying pan over a medium–high heat. Add the prawns and scallops. Stir-fry for 2–3 minutes until the prawns have just turned pink.

Pour the seafood over the pasta and toss well to mix. Sprinkle with the basil. Serve immediately.

index